Planting Peace

Gwendolyn Hooks
Margaux Carpentier

Crocodile Books, USA
An imprint of Interlink Publishing Group, Inc.
www.interlinkbooks.com

First published in 2021 by
Crocodile Books
An imprint of Interlink Publishing Group, Inc.
46 Crosby Street, Northampton, MA 01060
www.interlinkbooks.com

Published simultaneously in the UK by Wayland, an
imprint of Hachette Children's Group

Managing Editor: Victoria Brooker
Designer: Anthony Hannant, Little Red Ant
Consultant: Dr. Jane Irungu

10 9 8 7 6 5 4 3 2 1

MIX
Paper from
responsible sources
FSC® C104740

Printed and bound in China

Library of Congress Cataloging-in-Publication data:
Names: Hooks, Gwendolyn, author. | Carpentier, Margaux,
    illustrator.
Title: Planting peace : the story of Wangari Maathai / Gwendolyn
    Hooks ; illustrated by Margaux Carpentier.
Description: Northampton, MA : Crocodile Books, 2021. |
    Includes index.
Identifiers: LCCN 2020054229 | ISBN 9781623718855 (hardback)
Subjects: LCSH: Maathai, Wangari—Juvenile literature. | Tree
    planters (Persons)—Kenya—Biography—Juvenile literature. |
    Green Belt Movement (Society : Kenya)—Juvenile literature.
    | Women environmentalists—Kenya—Biography—Juvenile
    literature. | Women conservationists—Kenya—Biography—
    Juvenile literature. | Women politicians—Kenya—Biography—
    Juvenile literature. | Women's rights—Kenya—Juvenile literature.
    | Nobel Prize winners—Biography—Juvenile literature. | Women
    Nobel Prize winners—Biography—Juvenile literature.
Classification: LCC SB63.M22 H66 2021 | DDC 333.72092 [B]—dc23
LC record available at https://lccn.loc.gov/2020054229

Foreword

As a little girl growing up in Kenya, it dawned on me that Wangari Maathai was one of the most learned and respected women in my community. People would talk about her humble background and her path to becoming the first woman to get a PhD in East Africa. It wowed me. I was drawn to her journey and excited that one day, maybe one day, I could get my PhD, too.

Although I am no Wangari Maathai, it's easy to see myself in this story. From Central Kenya, to Kansas, to the academy, I followed the same path two decades ago. It's women like Wangari Maathai that showed Kenyan women like myself the way. She made the little village girls and boys who could hardly speak English believe that it was possible to be anything we aspired to be.

This book maps out that path and unfolds Wangari's path to greatness in a seamless and beautiful narrative. I hope that everyone who reads this book can take away one lesson—believe in yourself. Regardless of your background, you too can change the world.

Jane Irungu, PhD. University of Oklahoma

Wangari Maathai   Jane Irungu

Author's note

When the book editor approached me about Wangari's story, I did a little research and quickly decided, yes! I want young readers to know and understand her devotion to a better environment for our world. Reading about Wangari's fascinating life made me realize we all have passions and gifts. They differ from person to person. Hers was focused on improving the environment so others could live healthy and fulfilling lives, especially children.

As you turn the last page, think about what you can do to keep our environment productive and clean. Remember Wangari's selflessness. Remember how a small tree seedling can grow into a tree that will provide shade, food, clean water, and beauty for people just like you.

Gwendolyn Hooks

Acknowledgement

I am extremely grateful for Dr. Jane Irungu's willingness to read my manuscript and answer questions about Kenya. She is originally from Kenya and, like Wangari, attended college in the United States. Both earned degrees in Kansas, at different schools. Now she is a professor at the University of Oklahoma, about 30 minutes from my home. Because of her, I now understand the difference between maize flour porridge and ugali and so much more.

Thank you, Dr. Jane Irungu.

Contents

The fig trees

Wangari made her way through the forest to collect firewood for her family. She was at home in the forest and looked forward to gathering the wood. It heated the water her family used for washing clothes, cleaning their home, and cooking their meals.

She enjoyed her peaceful walks, but she always remembered her mother's warning: do not gather wood from fig trees. She knew the ones her mother meant. Their roots spread out and burrowed deep into the ground holding the tree firmly in place. Birds sheltered in the trees eating the tasty figs.

Why couldn't she have a taste of figs too, Wangari wondered. Or use its branches to heat water for their dinner? One day, she would learn how their lives depended on the trees. But as a young girl, she had no reason to think that the trees would not be there forever.

Welcome to the world, Wangari

On April 1, 1940, in a small village in Kenya, a baby girl was born into the clan of leaders, Anjiru. She was of the Kikuyu community. Her parents named her Wangari.

Wangari grew up among luscious green shrubs and tall, leafy fig trees. The nearby stream's water was clear, clean and fresh. It was the community's water. Arrowroots, bananas, and sugarcane grew along its banks.

Sometimes the stream was full of tiny, round beads. They were so beautiful, sparkling in the water, that Wangari tried to catch them. But no matter how hard she tried, they slithered and slipped away. Then one day, the round beads disappeared from the stream and something new appeared.

Now she saw rounded bodies with tails swimming peacefully in the stream. Before long, they also disappeared and suddenly frogs appeared hopping in and out of the water! Wangari had witnessed the magical secret life of frogs and her lifelong fascination with nature began.

A garden of her own

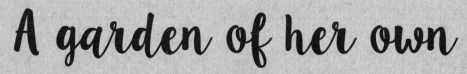

One rainy season, Wangari's mother gave her a plot of land. Her mother taught her how to care for it, but it would be hers to till, tend and grow vegetables. Wangari planted sweet potatoes, beans, corn, and millet that she would grind into flour.

Wangari was curious and often pulled up her plants while they were tiny to check on their progress. What were the seeds doing under the dirt? Were they growing quickly or slowly? If her mother saw her, she would say, "No, no, no. You can't remove them. You have to cover them. You have to let them do this all by themselves. Soon they will all come above the ground." And to Wangari's amazement, they did.

The natural world continued to fascinate Wangari.
She watched her plants grow, noticed the changes from
season to season, and how each plant grew according
to its own clock.

School surprise

One day, one of her brothers asked their mother: "Why doesn't Wangari go to school like us?" Their uncle, Kamunya, sent his sons and daughters to school. But most girls didn't attend school. Wangari thought her mother would surely say no. Her mother still had young children at home. Who would watch them for her? Who would pay the school fee of one shilling and 50 cents?

What a surprise when her mother announced, "There's no reason *why not*." Her mother had made an unusual decision on her own. She didn't consult any of the men in the family, not even Wangari's father. She decided her daughter would learn just like her sons.

Before she knew it, Wangari was enrolled in the Presbyterian Ihithe Primary School. She had no idea what to expect. On the first day, her cousin Jono walked her to school. Suddenly he stopped. He asked if she knew how to read and write? Wangari did not. Jono pulled out a pencil and wrote something on a sheet of paper. Wangari's eyes widened. It was a miracle! She had never seen written words before!

"This is what you will learn in school," he told her. Wangari never forgot that moment—the power of writing and reading.

The miracle of learning

Ihithe Primary School wasn't fancy—a dirt floor and mud walls under a tin roof. A wood fire warmed them during the cool months of June, July, and August.

Over the next four years, Wangari studied math, geography, and another African language. At home, her community spoke Kikuyu. At school she learned Kiswahili, the language spoken by the Swahili people. Best of all, she learned the miracle of reading and writing.

She also studied English. Her English teacher would walk to the door. This is a door, he announced. He walked to a wall. This is a wall, he told them. Soon they learned all the parts of a building.

When Wangari's time at primary school was over, she thought her learning was over. She knew Kenyan girls were not highly educated, if at all. Their role was to take care of the family. She would miss her new friends, her teachers, and learning.

More surprises

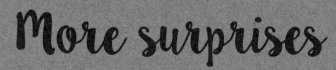

Wangari's mother surprised her again. Wangari would continue her education at St. Cecilia's. Attending this school would mean a big change in Wangari's life because St. Cecilia's was a boarding school. Wangari would live at St. Cecilia's. She was only 11 years old. Could she bear to leave her family and the huge fig trees and her gurgling stream of frogs? But the chance to learn more about the world outside her village filled her heart and head. She would study hard. She would show what Kenyan girls could accomplish.

Her mother gave her a short haircut so it would be easier to keep neat away from home. It was time to leave home and walk with her cousin to her new school. On the day-long journey, crossing a footbridge over the swirling Chania River, Wangari noticed the many plants growing along its banks. It reminded her of home and calmed her nerves.

Eating fire

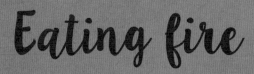

Wangari slipped easily into the school's routine. But sometimes there were mistakes, mostly due to language. Everyone in Kenyan schools had to speak and write in English. For some, this rule resulted in misunderstandings. One student wrote a letter to her family saying she ate fire. In her language, she meant they were having a great time.

Fire was not on the menu. For breakfast, they ate maize flour porridge. For lunch, it was corn and beans. And at 5 pm, they ate their evening meal—ugali (a mush of cornmeal) with vegetables.

Wangari was an excellent student at St. Cecilia's and graduated at the top of her class. It was time to move on to Loreto Girls' High School.

19

Fly away

After working hard for two years at Loreto Girls' High School, graduation was near and school would soon be behind her. For young Kenyan ladies graduating in 1959, there were two choices open to them— teaching or nursing. Neither was appealing to Wangari. Surely, there was another option? Wangari found it!

The Kennedy Foundation had set aside money for African students to attend college in the United States. Besides paying their college fees, the fund also paid for their transportation. The United States was so far away from her family and friends. She would not have money for visits home. Wangari's teachers considered her one of their most promising students. They encouraged her to accept the challenge. Soon she was on a plane heading towards the United States of America.

The trip was long, but Wangari saw places she had read about only in geography and history classes. The never-ending Sahara Desert was awe-inspiring. She dined on frog's legs when they stopped in Luxembourg. Frog's legs! She hadn't known that people ate frogs. *Why not try them?* She was learning so much and she hadn't even started college yet!

Cockroaches and quails

At St. Scholastica College in Atchison, Kansas, Wangari decided to study biology, chemistry, and German. The teachers were encouraging like the ones at home and, after four years, she graduated with a Bachelor of Science degree.

Keen to keep studying, Wangari moved to Pittsburgh, to take advanced biology classes. However, when her professor suggested she study the life cycle of the cockroach, she had to object. She imagined cockroaches crawling all over her.

Her professor suggested she study Japanese quail instead. It wasn't a large bird so it would be easy to handle and it did not resemble a cockroach! Her assignment was to learn the purpose of its pineal gland and how the gland developed during the quail's lifetime. It meant she had to explain what the gland was all about. Wangari did it and earned her Master's degree in biology.

Kenya and Kenyatta

In the USA, Wangari led a peaceful life compared to unsettling news she was hearing from home. In 1963, after many years of British rule, Kenya gained independence. Jomo Kenyatta became the country's first president. He was Kikuyu just like her. He gave Kikuyu people the better jobs. He banned anyone from voting against him. After many British people left Kenya, President Kenyatta gave their land to Kikuyus. This angered other communities. It was unfair. After all, they were Kenyans too.

Wangari listened to the president on the radio encouraging Kenyans to return to the rural areas. Grow coffee and tea like the British, he urged them. He believed selling those crops would help Kenya prosper. Would it?

Wangari had been offered a job working with a zoology professor at University College in Nairobi. It was time to return home. What would Kenya be like when she returned? Would Kenya look the same? Would it feel the same? Wangari couldn't wait to find out.

25

Homecoming

Wangari had mailed her family a letter notifying them about her upcoming arrival in Nairobi. She knew they would be busy and didn't expect them to make the long and expensive journey from their rural home.

But, to her astonishment, her beloved family was waiting for her as she stepped off the plane. Her heart was full of love and excitement to see them. After six years, Wangari was back home at last.

A new job

Excitement bubbled through Wangari as she reported to her new job. She was going to teach college students and study the desert locust with the zoology professor. But her excitement lasted only a few minutes.

The professor told her she didn't have a job. Wangari couldn't believe it! She showed him the letter he wrote to her offering her the position. The professor had given the job to a man who was not from Wangari's Kikuyu community. The man was from the same community as the professor. It wasn't fair. They were all Kenyans.

Wangari realized her new life wouldn't easily fall into place, but she did not give up hope of working at the university. Soon after, Wangari found a job in the veterinary department.

Sometimes she thought about her promised job that had disappeared. Kenya had survived British rule—now that they ruled themselves, why not treat everyone fairly even if they were from different communities?

Dry, dusty land

As part of her work, Wangari traveled through rural areas. She noticed the clear rivers and streams of her youth were now muddy. Instead of plentiful grass, she saw dusty land. Instead of fat cows, she saw bony ones. She noticed how the environment affected the health of its animals. Any remaining grass had few nutrients, not nearly enough for cows to grow normally and produce milk and meat.

Even more devastating, children looked as if they lacked nutrients, just like the cows and crops in their fields. The children were suffering from malnutrition. This was unheard of when she was a child. They always had enough food to eat. Their gardens produced nutritious food. She and her brothers and sisters grew up strong and healthy. What had happened since she had flown to the United States?

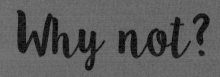

Why not?

There were more signs of a poor environment at her family's rural homestead. Land once thick with trees was now full of tea and coffee plants. Even her beautiful fig tree had been cut down to make room for coffee plants. She was heartsick.

Tea and coffee plants were draining the soil of nutrients. The plants were short and leafy with small branches. Rural people could not get enough money from selling these plants to pay for enough nutritious food for their children. Their homes didn't have electricity or gas. They still cooked over open fires and firewood was scarce.

People needed a better way to earn money for school fees and clothes. Wangari was determined to find a way help those who suffered. Could she do it? *Why not?*

33

The trouble with trees

Wangari believed if something was truly important, then you must do something about it. The stream with its mysterious frogs was important to her. The fig trees of her youth were important to her. The soil with its rich nutrients that allowed her vegetable garden to grow was important to her. Her family and all Kenyan people were important to her. To see the devastation that had occurred over the years broke her heart.

Could she help? She thought about her mother's strength. *Why not?* She realized cutting down most or all of the trees caused the problem. Normally, tree roots grabbed the soil and held it tight, keeping the soil from washing away in heavy rains. Without tree roots, there was nothing to hold on to the soil.

Tree roots would filter pollutants, such as farm animal waste, out of the water as it flowed downward into the earth. Land once thick with trees was now a desert. The trees that had once captured farm waste pollutants were gone and the waste was free to run into streams and rivers. Their water was no longer safe to drink.

A simple solution

As Wangari studied the problem, she realized the answer was simple. Plant trees! Trees would hold the soil in place and people would be able to plant vegetables again. They could eat what they planted instead of having to buy all their food and they could sell any extra vegetables to make money. If she could tell people about the problem and encourage them to plant trees, then maybe the problem could be reversed. But she needed help.

Wangari proposed a tree planting program to the National Council of Kenyan Women (NCKW). They understood the needs of rural women and would want to help them. Women who lived in the rural areas didn't have access to jobs. They didn't have opportunities to earn money. They struggled to provide enough food for their children.

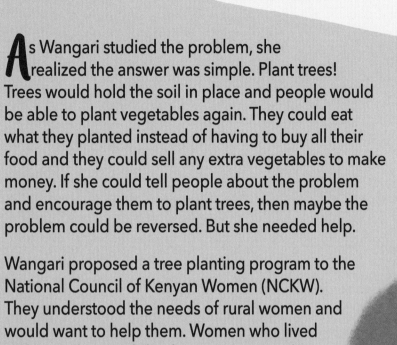

NCKW members had doubts about Wangari's tree planting idea, but that didn't stop Wangari. She talked and talked and, finally, they agreed to help.

Green Belt Movement

Wangari and NCKW planned a tree planting ceremony called *Save the Land Harambee* to raise awareness. Harambee means "Let's All Pull Together." Wangari wanted the different communities to understand everyone needed to work as one to help each other peacefully. It would be a challenge because of the president's policy of favoring the Kikuyu people and leaving out the other communities of Kenya.

The ceremony took place in Nairobi on June 5, 1977–World Environment Day. They planted seven trees in honor of seven Kenyans who had made a difference during their lifetime. The trees formed a rectangular area or belt of trees which led to the name, Green Belt Movement.

Why not work together?

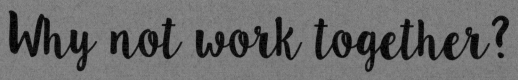

A few months later, the women of NCKW planted a second "green belt." This time, they planted seedlings on land owned by a group of rural women. Wangari suggested the NCKW travel throughout the rural areas to share the tree planting idea and give out seeds. She was told it wouldn't work. Women would need to teach women from other communities.

Communities don't get along. It would cause problems. Anger. Fights. Violence. They would never work together. Never!

Why not? Wangari understood the history of the different communities. Wangari did not believe in giving up, especially when lives of children depended on them. Her friends faced a determined Wangari who would not give up. NCKW gave in.

Fig tree seeds

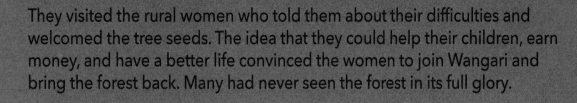

They visited the rural women who told them about their difficulties and welcomed the tree seeds. The idea that they could help their children, earn money, and have a better life convinced the women to join Wangari and bring the forest back. Many had never seen the forest in its full glory.

They planted seeds, watered them, and watched over them as if they were babies under their care. In those seeds, they saw a healthier and happy future for their families and themselves.

Only the beginning

Wangari organized groups of rural women to continue working on their own to improve their environment. Together, they envisioned a living forest, not acres of dusty soil. Wangari wanted them to see the vibrant trees of her youth. She wanted to see their children marvel at the life cycle of frogs in clear, clean, bubbling streams.

But then Wangari ran into a problem. NCKW couldn't provide all the seeds she needed. She asked the government's forestry department to donate seeds. At first, the department doubted that rural women would know how to plant and care for seeds. Wangari assured them they could do it. Women had been farmers for centuries. She called them foresters without diplomas.

Organizations donated money so Wangari could pay the women. They earned money once the seeds germinated and became seedlings. It was only pennies, but they gratefully accepted it and continued planting.

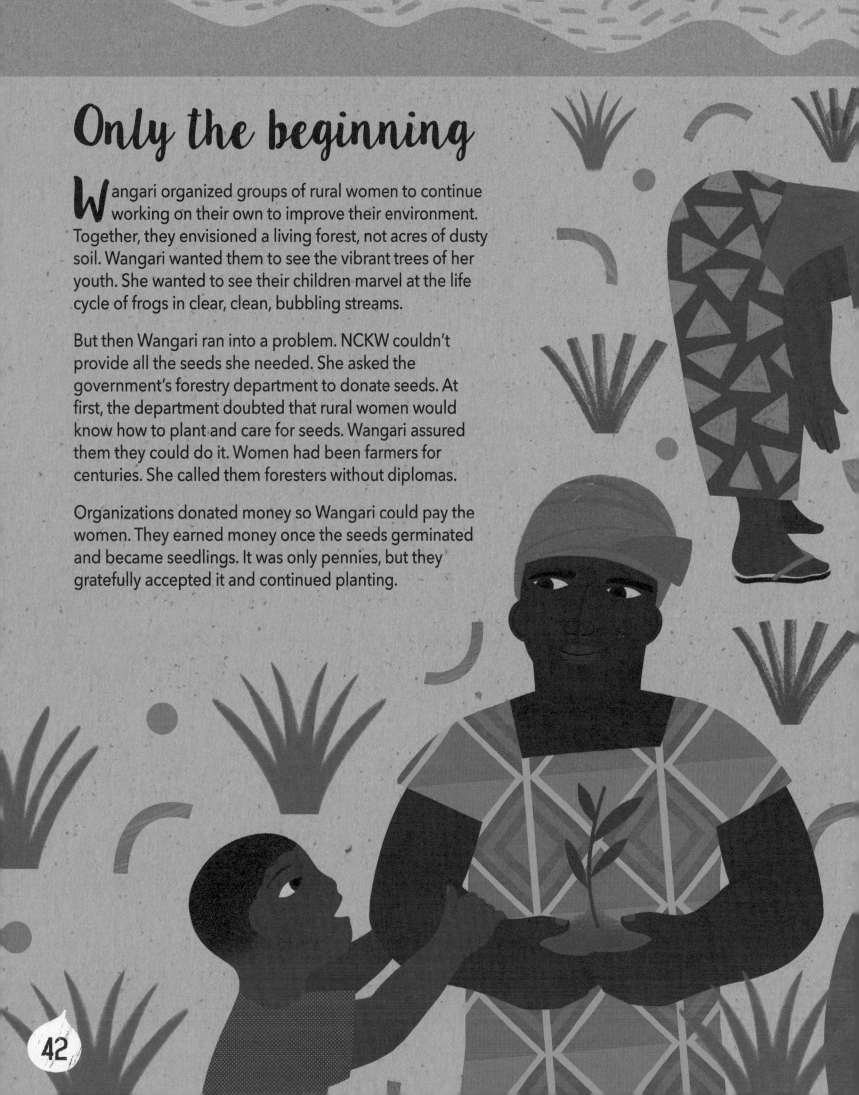

A growing idea

Soon the number of women in the Green Belt Movement grew and grew. The number of planted seeds grew. The number of trees in the forest grew. As time passed, streams gurgled with clean drinking water. The community could once again rely on home-grown foods. Their children were healthier. Government officials, like the foresters and other men who had laughed and chided them about planting seeds, were silenced.

As women worked within their own communities, they realized they shared the same problems as those in other communities. They began to reach out to them. They worked side by side.

They looked beyond the unfairness created by President Kenyatta's favoring the Kikuyu's with the most fertile land and better job opportunities. They focused on their children. They peaceably helped one another by digging together in the soil and planting trees.

Calling all communities

The simple idea of planting trees grew and grew. Other communities saw the results and joined the women. They wanted the best for their children, too. Across Kenya, women planted trees. Men began to help by volunteering their time to plant trees. Schools and churches joined the movement.

Everywhere Wangari traveled, she shared the importance of returning trees to the land and how it would change their lives and the lives of their children. Once this connection was understood, more and more men and women took part in the project. They became the roots of the movement and their efforts its leaves.

From losing to winning

After 12 years of teaching at the University of Nairobi, Wangari resigned to run for Parliament. She had noticed the misuse of the country's money. Those who protested the misuse were arrested and some were found dead. Newspapers were ordered not to print stories about government problems. Wangari hoped to bring fairness and openness to all Kenyans.

But she lost the election and she lost her teaching position. The university had given it to someone else. She was down, but not defeated. Wangari turned her full attention to the Green Belt Movement. She began to receive awards for her work.

1983 Woman of the Year in Kenya

1984 Right Livelihood Award

1986 Medal from the Better World Society

1988 Windstar Award

1989
Woman of the
World Award

Wangari and Uhuru Park

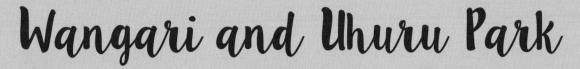

News about Wangari's work spread throughout Kenya. She became known as a woman who stood up for others and their environment.

One day in 1989, a university student visited Wangari. He was clearly upset and needed advice. He told her about the government's plans for Nairobi's largest city park, Uhuru Park. It would soon have a skyscraper! This beautiful park, with its green lawns and trees, lake and children's playground, would become home to a sixty-story building, a parking lot for two thousand cars, and a statue of the current president, Daniel Moi.

Wangari thought it was foolish to ruin a beautiful green space with a concrete building. It would cost 200 million dollars to build it. Kenya's government could not afford to pay and would need to get a loan. Why borrow money to ruin a city park?

Peaceful protest

Wangari decided she must do something to stop the building from being built. Women and men joined, but mostly rural women.

Wangari and others in the movement wrote letters of protest to the government. The government ignored the letters.

Wangari wrote letters to the newspapers. Nairobi's citizens were not happy to learn their beautiful, peaceful park would soon become home to a skyscraper. They also wrote letters to the government, newspapers, and magazines.

News of the skyscraper spread around the world.
Finally, the publicity was too much and the
government abandoned the program.

House arrest and prison

One day, Wangari learned about President Moi's latest idea. He had decided to turn the government over to the army. This would stop anyone from running against him in the elections and therefore he would always be the president. Wangari and her friends spoke out against him. Police tried to enter her house, but she would not let them. They guarded her home so she couldn't leave.

Then one day, they broke in and arrested her. She was charged with spreading hateful rumors and being disloyal toward the government. If the court found her guilty, it could result in the death penalty. Senators from the United States followed the story and spoke out against the Kenyan government. It was not treating its people fairly. Wangari was released.

The fight for freedom and peace

In 1992, Wangari's reputation for helping others and fighting for justice led to a group of mothers asking Wangari to help with the release of their sons from jail. The young men had protested peacefully against the government. They wanted a two-party political system. They believed more than one person should be allowed to run for president. But even after a new rule allowed more than one person on the ballot, the men were not released from jail.

The mothers and Wangari met on a corner of Uhuru Park. They called it Freedom Corner. Then they walked to the attorney general's office and asked for the men's release. He said he would look into it. The women returned to the park to wait for an answer. None came.

The women began a hunger strike to help publicize their cause. They took turns not eating. On the third day, police fired tear gas at them and beat them with batons. Wangari was hit and lost consciousness. She was rushed to the hospital. She awoke with a black eye and a large lump on her head. The women didn't give up. Instead, they moved into a church for greater safety.

The women continued their peaceful protest and hunger strike until the men were released a year after their arrest. Their protest worked!

Nobel Peace Prize

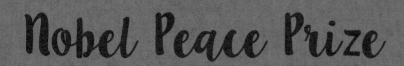

In 2004, Wangari Maathai won the Nobel Peace Prize. She said the news hit her like a thunder bolt and left her speechless.

Some asked, what does planting trees have to do with peace? She didn't need to answer with complicated words. A trip to the rural areas to watch women, men, and children from various communities working side by side was the answer.

Different communities had opposing views and they often fought each other because of these differences. But Wangari showed how planting trees helped everyone and brought communities together. It didn't matter if they belonged to the Kikuyu community or the Embu community. She planted trees with women and men from all communities. And those women and men showed others how to plant trees.

The Green Belt Movement didn't stop in the rural areas of Wangari's home country. It spread across Africa and to countries worldwide. Wangari's simple idea had spread the seeds of peace.

Wangari's gift to the world

The Green Belt Movement was a long walk for Wangari. She believed in moving forward, step by step, when others doubted her. She believed trees would help answer the needs of rural communities. Her life story proved it to be true.

Her belief in the women of Kenya proved that, with the proper knowledge and tools, people can make the world a better place for their children, themselves, and the whole community.

Wangari's fascination and passion for the environment is a lasting legacy in Kenya. She died on September 25, 2011. But Wangari's idea took root and grew and grew and is still growing with branches around the world.

Why not
plant trees?

Why not plant peace?

61

Glossary

biology the study of all living things such as lions and cockroaches and people

death penalty a sentence of death as punishment for a crime

diploma an official piece of paper stating that a student has earned a degree or finished a course of study. High schools, colleges, and universities give out diplomas

election the process of choosing a person for office by voting

environment the natural world we live in

forester people who work looking after forests

government the power to make laws and important decisions that control or affect all people living in a community

graduate a person who has finished studying at high school or college

homestead a house and the land and buildings that are around it

hunger strike a refusal to eat, as by a prisoner or protester, until certain conditions or demands are met

maize flour porridge a breakfast dish, made of corn meal flour and cooked to a light consistency

malnutrition the condition of not having enough food or not having the right kind of food for good health

millet seeds from a type of grass used for food

miracle a wonderful or amazing event or thing

Nobel Peace Prize an international prize awarded every year for achievements in, and the promotion of peace

nutritious providing a large amount of vitamins, minerals, or other nutrients

Parliament a group of people who make the laws for a country

policy a set of rules or a plan that is used as a guide for action

rainy season a season of high rainfall

rural having to do with country life

seedling a young plant grown from a seed